The Pope's Exorcist

The editors of Sophia Institute Press

The Pope's Exorcist

101 Questions about Fr. Gabriele Amorth

SOPHIA INSTITUTE PRESS
Manchester, New Hampshire

Cover design: Updatefordesign Studio

Cover image: Catholic priest walking
(651080735) (c) Grant Faint / www.gettyimages.com

Sophia Institute Press
Box 5284, Manchester, NH 03108
1-800-888-9344

www.SophiaInstitute.com

Sophia Institute Press® is a registered trademark of Sophia Institute.

paperback ISBN 978-1-64413-953-0

ebook ISBN 978-1-64413-954-7

Library of Congress Control Number: 2023930597

Foreword

Starting out as an exorcist years ago, I "grew up" on the writings of Fr. Gabriele Amorth. There was little else printed on the subject. I devoured everything of his I could find. He was a pioneer of sorts, reintroducing the Catholic world to a long-forgotten and sometimes hidden reality.

His approach was direct and uncomplicated. His writings are not abstract theological tomes but rather the sharing of his personal experience. After years in exorcism ministry, I have found that much of what he says resonates with my own experience. In fact, as I speak to exorcists around the world, it is striking how similar our experiences are. It confirms the reality of what we face, in Fr. Amorth's day and in our own. The basic realities of God, Satan, and human beings have not changed.

One of the attributes that strikes the reader about Fr. Amorth is his simple, matter-of-fact plainness. He was not flashy. He was not given to extremes or showmanship. Fr. Amorth did not claim to have special charisms. He presented himself simply as a priest with faculties as an exorcist who diligently and faithfully performed his ministry.

It is said that every day, for nearly thirty years, he engaged in casting out demons from the afflicted. He never took time off. He felt an urgent and compelling sense of mission. Even when he grew frail and sick in God's service, only upon the direct command of a superior did he retire.

One reason for his unceasing dedication to the ministry was his awareness that there were few exorcists in Italy and a dearth of exorcists in the world as a whole. Some countries had not a single exorcist, which is the case even today. Thus, people regularly came to him for help from France, Austria, Germany, Switzerland, Spain, and England.

While the Holy See has asked every diocese around the world to appoint an exorcist, many still have not. Fr. Amorth saw this as a serious and culpable failure of leadership. He was appalled when he encountered bishops and priests who did not believe in the reality of Satan and his action in this world. I share his distress. Could the Scriptures and Church teaching and tradition be any clearer?

Fr. Amorth's pastoral practice was solidly rooted in the teachings of the Catholic Church and the truths given to us in the Word of God. His ministry was centered on Christ who has definitively smashed Satan's kingdom. He was confident in the authority and power given to the Church when confronting the Evil One. He taught exorcists, and indeed all Christians, to be fearless in our encounters with Satan and his minions. He humorously stated, "When the Devil sees me, he poops his pants."

We owe a debt to Fr. Amorth. He was courageous in casting out demons. He was also courageous in his witness to the full truth of the Gospels and Church teaching. His reflections are as timely and relevant today as they were when he first penned them. I hope that you find encouragement, inspiration, and insight, as I and many others have, in his life and work. I also hope that in reading these pages you find that the heart of this kind and faith-filled man touches your heart and brings you much peace.

Msgr. Stephen J. Rossetti Ph.D. D.Min.
Research Associate Professor, Catholic University of America
Exorcist, Archdiocese of Washington

Contents

Foreword v

Part One:

About Fr. Amorth 3

Part Two:

The Devil and Demons 27

Part Three:

The Ministry of Exorcism 51

Short Biography of Fr. Amorth 81

Resources 85

Prayers. 95

The Pope's Exorcist

PART ONE

About Fr. Amorth

1. When was Fr. Amorth born?

He was born in Moderna on May 1, 1925, and he was the youngest of five sons. His parents were Mario and Giuseppina Amorth; Father described them as deeply religious.

2. Was he a good student?

No, he was not — by his own admission! As a boy, he only ever aimed to get a sixty: a grade just high enough to pass. He was more interested in sports. Fr. Amorth was an avid fencer and gymnast. He also enjoyed rock climbing, a passion inspired by Pope Pius XI, after whom a peak in the Apennines is named.

3. What did he do before he joined the priesthood?

He and all of his brothers were drafted into the Italian Army during World War II. However, Father chose to fight for the Resistance against the Fascist government. After World War II, he was awarded a gold star for military valor. After the war, he briefly dabbled in law (like his father) and politics. He was a high-ranking member of the Christian Democratic Party and even helped Italian Prime Minister Giulio Andreotti draft the country's new constitution. He also wrote for several Catholic publications, as well as some papers aligned with the CDP.

4. Why did he become a priest?

Fr. Amorth began to discern his priestly vocation when he was twelve years old. He was deeply influenced by St. Pius of Pietrelcina (better known as Padre Pio), whom he visited every year for twenty-six years. Eventually, St. Pius became his spiritual director.

After Fr. Amorth's stint in law and politics, he decided to answer his calling to the priesthood. Because of his deep devotion to St. Gabriel of Our Lady of Sorrows, he originally planned to join the Passionists. Eventually he was invited to join the Society of St. Paul — also known as the Paulines — by the order's founder, Blessed Giacomo Alberione.

5. Was the transition from politician-journalist to exorcist-priest difficult?

Certainly. Fr. Amorth was thirty-two when he was ordained and didn't become an exorcist until he was in his sixties. Eventually, this new ministry forced him to stop writing regularly. In time, he even had to give up regular preaching. He devoted himself full-time to performing exorcisms and training new exorcists. Throughout his career, he was notorious for criticizing the bishops for not investing enough priests with the ministry of exorcism.

But Fr. Amorth also drew great personal benefits from his ministry. It deepened his supernatural faith — how could it not? — and helped him to grow in charity. He liked to quote St. John Chrysostom: "The devil is the sanctifier of souls." ("Against his will!" Father added.)

6. Was Fr. Amorth always sensitive to supernatural activity?

Surprisingly, no! In an interview with Vatican journalist Marco Tosatti, Father confessed that before he was ordained, demons "never occupied my thoughts very much. Yes, I knew that there *was* a devil, and I believed in the Gospel.... I never heard anyone speak of the existence of exorcists.... In those times, many priests practically never spoke of the devil, possessions or exorcisms."

7. Who most influenced his ministry as an exorcist?

Fr. Amorth considered Fr. Matteo La Grua to be the greatest exorcist in the world. Fr. La Grua was about ten years older than Fr. Amorth. He served as exorcist for the Diocese of Palermo for over thirty years, and he authored dozens of books.

As a new exorcist, Fr. Amorth was "apprentice" to Fr. Candido Amantini, whom Fr. Amorth called a saint.

He was also deeply devoted to Bl. Francisco Palau, O.C.D. Fr. Palau was a Carmelite friar who felt the bishops were neglecting the ministry of exorcism. Fr. Palau had planned to start a new religious order just for exorcists when his local bishop forbade him to practice the ministry of exorcism at all.

Bl. Francisco Palau inspired Fr. Amorth's belief that the Church had an urgent duty to restore the ministry of exorcism from three centuries of "bestial" neglect (see question sixty-five).

8. Where did Fr. Amorth work?

Here's how the journalist Tracy Wilkinson describes his workplace in her book on Vatican exorcists:

> Father Amorth receives his tormented flock and celebrates exorcisms in the building that hosts his office and accommodations and that of his confreres of the Society of St. Paul. His room is always distant from the street, so that no one can

hear the screams. "Otherwise the police arrive," says Amorth with a hint of a smile.

The walls are a sea green, broken off here and there by some cracks in the plaster. In all, the room measures about nine feet by fifteen. There are five or six straight back chairs leaning against the walls and a lightly padded chair with a vinyl covering where, Amorth said, patients who do not present themselves in very critical conditions can accommodate themselves. The helpers are seated on other chairs, and among them there may be priests, relatives of the patient and family members, or the assistants who help to control them. Amorth also often turns to laymen, followers of the Catholic Charismatic Renewal, who participate with their prayers. "Many prayers are needed," he says. The more unstable or sick patients that may have to be tied down with straps are stretched out on a small bed with padding, similar to those used in medical offices. Amorth showed me the straps that are used for this purpose. Violence is always an eventuality; therefore, there are always assistants. Few priests practice exorcism alone.

> On the walls of the room for exorcism, Amorth has attached eight crucifixes, some images of Our Lady and a picture of St. Michael the Archangel. A small statuette of the Virgin Mary, our Lady of Fatima, is placed on a small table in a corner. There are also images of Pope John Paul II, of the famous Italian saint Padre Pio; Amorth's mentor, Father Candido, and Father Giacomo Alberione, founder of the congregation of the Society of St. Paul. (*The Vatican's Exorcists: Driving Out the Devil in the 21st Century*, 2007)

9. What was Father's daily schedule?

One of his patients described Fr. Amorth's day thus:

> Among the fixed collaborators, there was Father Stanislaw and at least three or four laymen that constituted a prayer group and assisted at restraining the patient. Each morning he began at 8:50 with the blessing of the water, salt, and oil, brought by a group of persons that evidently had a great need of it, in addition there were always three or four persons that profited from it by asking for a quick blessing. The morning exorcism began at 9:00 a.m. with a half hour pause between

appointments for the paperwork. Each morning there were five appointments, mostly cases that were already known that came from Rome or somewhere in Lazio, although at times they came from adjacent regions, from the North of Italy and from abroad. In some rare cases, other prelates pleaded for appointments for their congregants, claiming the impossibility of finding a good exorcist in their dioceses.

The atmosphere of the little rectangular room where the exorcisms were performed was strange, nearly surreal; one gained access through a small door of wood and opaque glass. As soon as you entered your glance was drawn to a worn-out armchair in brown velvet that served the less agitated patients. The ceiling was high, and the walls were white but a bit soiled in spots. Two windows provided illumination and during the hot weather warmed the ambience. But during the winter it is rather cold.

Under the window there was a small bed with a faded green cover and a thick blanket at the base where the patient forced to use it — the vast majority — would place his feet. Under the bed was a wooden box containing the tapes and belts used to tie the more robust, generally men, in order to prevent them from doing harm during the prayer. I recall little of what happened during my attendance, but thinking back, I can now say that some people would not be able to be held firm even with six or seven volunteers if they had not been tied; therefore, it is a very useful precaution done for their own good.

On another wall of the same room there is a bookshelf with diverse religious books, a Roman missal, some theological works and a biography of some of the saints. During the exorcisms, some folding chairs are brought into the room from the adjoining antechamber, which functions as a waiting room for the persons scheduled for exorcisms during the morning. The seats serve not only for Father Amorth and the relatives and friends of the persons exorcized, but also for the persons that assist, their relations, and the permanent helpers.... In addition there was Francesco, and now and then other laymen, brothers, seminarians and priests from every part of the world who wished to participate in order to learn and to see what happens and especially to help through their prayers.

10. What were Fr. Amorth's "tools of the trade"?

According to Wilkinson, Father carried "an old briefcase containing a silver crucifix and a wooden crucifix, a silver aspergillum for spraying holy water, and a phial of consecrated oil. In addition, he uses a purple priestly stole and a book of prayers with the official formulas for the exorcism." Fr. Amorth also found images of Pope St. John Paul II to be extremely efficacious. "The demons become very irritable before him," he said.

11. Was he afraid of the demons he fought against?

"I have never been afraid," Father said. "Not even at the beginning! Never! I always say it is the devil who is afraid of me."

Father had a deep, perhaps miraculous, trust in Our Lady. When he began his ministry as an exorcist, he begged her to wrap him in her mantle. And from the very outset, he believed that she would keep him safe from all harm.

And she did. That's why, during a television appearance, he announced, "When the devil sees me, he poops his pants."

12. What was Fr. Amorth's first exorcism like?

Father's first exorcism was dramatic, even by industry standards. For most of the exorcism, the demon was unresponsive. However, after Father prayed the *Praecipio tibi* (I command you), the demoniac began to calm down. At that point, Father cried, "Unclean spirit! Whoever you are and all your companions who possess this servant of God … I command you: tell me your name, the day and the hour of your damnation."

The demon possessing the man replied, "I am Lucifer."

13. Did Fr. Amorth have any close collaborators in his ministry?

Many priests and laymen assisted Fr. Amorth over the course of his career. A lot of those priests considered themselves his "spiritual sons." He rejected this title, but only because he felt they overestimated his own wisdom in forming them. ("I have nothing to teach," he said — which surely was Father's modesty getting the better of him!)

Father's closest collaborator was a priest named Fr. Stanislaw.

14. Who was Fr. Stanislaw?

As a young Passionist, Fr. Stanislaw struggled with a belief in demonic possession. He believed in the devil and his fallen angels, but not in their ability to take control of a human's body. So, a friend suggested he pay a visit to Fr. Amorth. From that moment on, he began to assist Fr. Amorth with his ministry:

> I do not know how to explain it, but nearly from the first day of my collaboration with Father Gabriele, he told me many times that he saw in me the priest sent by Mary to succeed him. He said to me, "I want you to take my place when I am no longer here."

The Diocese of Rome appeared to resist their collaboration, however. When Fr. Amorth took a leave of absence from his exorcism ministry, Fr. Stanislaw was also ordered to desist:

> Perhaps someone at the top of the ecclesial hierarchy thought that I shared Father Amorth's opinion that bishops who do not nominate exorcists are living in mortal sin. In fact, on this I am in total agreement with him, and he always said it openly without too many scruples. Clearly, his speaking directly made him dangerous for the men of the Church who did not believe in the extraordinary action of the Devil.

Stanislaw was a true spiritual son to Amorth, and Amorth was a true spiritual father to Stanislaw:

> For me, he was a life model, like Mother Teresa of Calcutta, with whom I had worked among the poor. But I must say that the material or physical poverty that I have seen in the hospital or in the streets takes second place to the spiritual poverty that I see in afflicted individuals.

15. What was Fr. Amorth's most difficult case?

Fr. Amorth said his hardest case was a young woman named Anna from southern Italy. She would go into states of possession for up to twenty-seven hours straight. Whenever she tried to look at a priest, her eyes would roll into the back of her head. In fact, Fr. Amorth worked with Anna for over a decade, and the first time she ever saw his face was at his funeral.

When Fr. Amorth was forced to retire, Anna's case was taken over by Fr. Stanislaw. Amorth told his apprentice, "This is the most serious case I have ever had in my life as an exorcist. My dear son, you shall see signs of God following this person."

When Fr. Stanislaw last spoke of Anna, she had not been fully liberated of her demon. But "weekly prayers and an exorcism once a month allow her to lead a normal enough life."

16. What was Fr. Amorth's relationship with the Charismatic Renewal?

Fr. Amorth was an early and enthusiastic supporter of the Charismatic Renewal. The Renewal was a movement in the Catholic Church that emphasized a personal relationship with Jesus Christ and the gifts of the Holy Ghost.

A favorite practice of charismatics is spontaneous intercessory prayer, especially over those suffering from afflictions — be they physical, mental, or spiritual. That is why Father frequently drew his assistants from prayer groups associated with the Renewal.

However, he was also keenly aware of the potential for abuse. "It is extremely wise to be on guard for false charismatics," he warned. "There are many of them!" He continued:

> When these sensitives are persons of prayer and truly humble, they try to remain hidden; these are the positive signs. But if a person says, "I am a charismatic," then he has no charism. The charismatic is humble and has hidden gifts that God gives him. The Lord gives some charisms, and he would give many more if there was more faith. I think of *Lumen Gentium* of Vatican Council II, that says in number twelve: "Those who have charge over the Church [bishops] should judge the genuine and orderly use of these gifts, and it is especially their office not indeed to extinguish the Spirit, but to test all things and hold fast to what is good" (see 1 Thessalonians 5:12, 19–21).

Fr. Amorth also criticized the practice of "laying on of hands" by the laity. He believed this form of prayer has a very specific liturgical function reserved for the clergy. He said that laymen who lay hands on one another are "exalting themselves." Rather, he instructed, "At most, raise a hand towards the person for whom you are praying, but nothing more."

17. How many exorcisms did he perform?

Near the end of his life, Fr. Amorth estimated that he had performed sixty thousand exorcisms — though many patients required hundreds of appointments. At that time, he held about seventeen appointments per day, yet "before [that] there were many more," he confessed.

18. How often did his exorcisms require multiple sessions?

Father's preference was to perform one exorcism every day until the demonic presence was banished. At a minimum, he would see his patients at least once a week. Father estimated that a total of fifty exorcisms were required for the most serious cases.

19. How long did these sessions take?

Father would devote at least thirty minutes per day for each case, but some required more time. "If one goes into a trance, for instance, it is necessary to wait until he becomes conscious. And let us note that when patients return to themselves, they are cheerful, content, and feel healed. But they are not healed. After a few hours or days, they fall back into the same situation."

Another exorcist, known by the pseudonym Fr. Theophilus, told the *National Catholic Register* that a successful exorcism "may take them ninety days or eight months." He insisted that sessions must occur daily and that if a single day is missed, the process must start over.

20. Did Fr. Amorth wear any special medals or scapulars?

Father only wore two medals. One was a Miraculous Medal. The other was of Our Lady of Pompeii, which an aunt placed around his neck when he was born. "It has been reduced to a thin leaf," he said during an interview—yet he never took it off.

21. Was Fr. Amorth more than just an exorcist?

He was! In addition to his work as an exorcist, Father also taught at a Pauline high school, edited several Catholic magazines, and served as a spiritual director for several religious orders. He also served briefly as the Paulines' delegate for the region of Italy.

22. Was he famous in his own lifetime?

This elderly priest was something of a celebrity. "I rarely go out to preach, only on very special occasions," he once admitted, "and then I have people assailing me, trying to touch me; I am always surrounded by bodyguards for protection from people who wish to touch me. And I say: 'Come on, touch me, smell me—I stink of salami!'"

23. Did he ever encounter saints as well as demons?

Yes! Father told his friend (and fellow exorcist) Fr. Marcello Stanzione that he received visions of St. Benedict, St. Gabriel of Our Lady of Sorrows, and his mentor Padre Pio.

24. Where is Fr. Amorth buried?

His funeral was held at Queen of the Apostles (*Regina degli Apostoli*), a church in Rome associated with the Paulines. Over 1,500 people attended the Mass, which was concelebrated by over a hundred priests. A thousand more paid respects to his body when it lay in repose at the church.

25. What is Fr. Amorth's legacy?

In 1991, Fr. Amorth founded the International Association of Exorcists (IAE), the largest and most influential group of Catholic exorcists in the world. For many years, he also served as the IAE's president. In addition to his writings and formation of young priests, this remains his most enduring legacy on the ministry of exorcism.

26. What was Fr. Amorth's advice to priests?

He said, "Read the Gospel; believe in the Gospel! And again, read the Gospel; believe in the Gospel! In the Gospel, there is everything! In the Word of God, there is everything! It is necessary, however, to believe it — to read it and believe it."

27. What was his advice to young exorcists?

Fr. Amorth would tell newcomers, "There is always a result. Always. It is so easy for an exorcist to become discouraged when his tenth, twentieth, or fiftieth exorcism fails to heal the demoniac. But the fault may not be with the priest. It may be that the victim is not cooperating; it may be that God's appointed time for the liberation has not yet come. But the exorcist's prayers always do some good for his patient, as well as the patients' friends and families. So, never stop fighting."

28. Did Fr. Amorth ever film his exorcisms?

There is footage of Fr. Amorth performing several exorcisms in the film *The Devil and Father Amorth*. Several of these clips can be found on YouTube.

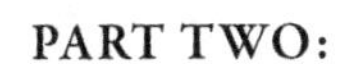

PART TWO:

The Devil and Demons

29. Why did God make the devil?

Strictly speaking, He didn't. Before God made humankind, He made the angels. According to Church teaching, about a third of those angels revolted. Their leader's name was Lucifer, whose name means "morning star." When Lucifer and his angels were defeated, St. Michael the Archangel cast them out of Heaven and into Hell. The fallen angels came to be known as demons, and Lucifer as Satan or the devil.

God never intended for the angels to be evil, though. As the Fourth Lateran Council explains, "The devil and other demons were created by God naturally good, but they became evil by their own doing."

30. Why did He create Hell?

God didn't create Hell either. "Hell" is anywhere that God is not. When the evil angels rebelled, they banished themselves from His presence. They cut themselves off from the source of all goodness, truth, and beauty.

Once, Fr. Amorth's mentor Fr. Candido taunted a demon by saying, "Come on, go. The Lord has prepared a nice, warm, heated box for you, where you shall not feel the cold, where you shall remain very warm."

"You do not know anything," the demon replied. "You do not understand anything. It is not He that created Hell. He did not even think of it. The existence of Hell was not in His plans!" The devil had Fr. Candido on that one!

Every time we sin, we too rebel against God. We cut ourselves off from Him. Therefore, those who die obstinate in their sins elect to spend eternity far away from God. They choose to spend eternity in the outer darkness with all those who rebel against God, including Satan and his angels.

31. What does the devil look like?

Nothing! The devil is a spiritual being. He has no body and therefore doesn't "look" like anything.

Traditional depictions of the devil with horns and goat legs are meant to emphasize that he is evil and perverse. And, indeed, if Satan *did* have a form, he would be unspeakably ugly — since he is almost completely separated from God, the source of all beauty and light. In this sense, the traditional depiction is useful.

However, it can become dangerous to become too attached to the traditional view of the devil. *Because* he is pure spirit, he can take any form he likes. He has been known to take the form of a beautiful woman, a friend, a relative, and even Jesus or Mary.

32. Why does Jesus call Satan "the ruler of this world"?

Christians believe that Satan convinced Adam and Eve to eat the forbidden fruit. This caused a rupture in all of God's creation. This is known as the *Fall of man*, though in fact all of nature "fell." God's perfect creation was made imperfect by our first parents' disobedience. That is why all humans die, for example — and not only humans, but also animals and plants and all living things.

Of course, God is the true ruler of everything in existence. He always has been; He always will be. And God will restore all creation — including mankind — in the end times. But because this world is currently subject to the power of sin and death, Jesus refers to Satan as its ruler or prince.

33. Are there really such things as Satanists?

Sadly, yes. Fr. Amorth estimated that there are thousands of Satanists around the world — a small but dangerous minority. Their creed has three points: "You can do as you wish, you obey no one, and you are yourself a god."

34. What does being a Satanist entail?

In order to become an initiated Satanist, one must first sign a contract (usually written in blood) pledging oneself to the devil for all eternity—both in this life and in the next.

Satanists also practice Black Masses. A naked woman is used for the altar; on her body, a consecrated Host (one stolen from a Catholic Church) is desecrated in the most obscene ways imaginable. The "altar" is then raped by all those in attendance, beginning with the officiant.

35. Why would anyone become a Satanist?

Men and women pledge themselves to Satan in exchange for certain favors, which are stipulated in the blood vow. There are usually three: sex, wealth, and power.

The third may refer to power in business or politics, but it almost always refers to *supernatural* power—for instance, the ability to see the future, cause illness, or make others fall in love (see question fifty-two).

36. What is a "LaVeyan Satanist"?

Anton LaVey (1930–1997) is the American founder of the Church of Satan and author of

The Satanic Bible. LaVey and his followers are nontheists; they do not believe in God or even the devil. Rather, for them, Satan is a symbol of freedom from Judeo-Christian morality. Its practitioners conduct elaborate rituals modeled closely after the traditional Black Mass.

While LaVeyan Satanists (ostensibly) do not believe in the devil, they are certainly an evil influence. Their invocations of demons can be efficacious, even if the Satanists themselves don't mean them to be. Dabbling in LaVeyan Satanism can also lead one to become a true Satanist. And, of course, those who worship evil for its own sake — especially in the guise of the devil — are almost certain to be damned.

37. What happens if one dabbles in Satanism out of curiosity — or even as a joke?

It makes no difference. If you invite Satan into your soul, he will accept — whether you were extending the invitation sincerely or not! The effects may not be as severe, or they may not manifest themselves as quickly. But there will always be consequences. Always.

38. Is there any truth to those conspiracy theories about high-level Satanists who secretly rule the world — and even the Church?

For what it's worth, Fr. Amorth believed strongly that Satanists move in very elite circles — particularly the Vatican. "Yes, there are many members of satanic sects also in the Vatican," he told the Vatican journalist Marco Tosatti. "I know it from persons who have referred them to me because they have a direct way of knowing it. And it is also often 'confessed' by the same demon that is under obedience in the exorcisms."

In another interview, Father added, "It is well known, unfortunately, that in the Vatican there are persons who are solely careerists; those who are seeking only the things below, not those above; and the devil profits from this, dazzling those who seek success and power."

39. What about rumors that the Freemasons are actually Satanists?

The first thing to note is that Catholics are forbidden to join any secret society. That includes any Freemasonic group, even those that go by other names, such as the Odd Fellows.

Some Catholics will make a distinction between Anglo-American Freemasonry and more radical groups that exist in Continental Europe. However, others do not deem any sort of Freemasonry safe. Fr. Amorth was among the latter. He called the Freemasons "the major support of satanic sects" and accused them of celebrating Black Masses, which involve the profanation of a consecrated Host.

40. Why did the devil take the form of a snake in the Garden of Eden?

Most Catholic sources deny that Satan himself became a snake, because God would not allow him in the Garden. Rather, he manipulated the snake into doing his evil will. This could be the first instance of demonic possession in history.

41. What are the signs of demonic possession?

Aversion to the Holy Eucharist and sacramentals is a telltale sign of demonic activity. Any physically repulsive behavior, such as drooling, is common in demoniacs. So are violent outbursts, both verbal and physical.

The sudden ability to speak a language one has never studied is also widely reported. For instance, an Italian peasant who can neither read nor write is suddenly able to discuss high-level theology in fluent English.

Demons will do unspeakable harm to their own "hosts" as well. According to Fr. Amorth, "Vexations are true and actual aggression, physical or psychological attacks that the demon works against a person. At times they result in scratches, burns, bruises, or, in the most serious cases, broken bones."

Many exorcists also report that their patients perform feats that for normal humans are physically impossible. Their heads rotate 180 degrees; their eyes roll into the backs of their heads; they levitate several feet off the ground.

For the most part, Hollywood has gotten this part right! One mistake they make is this: it is actually very difficult for the possessed to curse.

42. Can the demons read our thoughts?

No. This is one power they do not possess. However, they are extremely intelligent — far more intelligent than we are — and can intuit a great deal simply by watching us. If our eyes linger on women as they walk past us, the demons will realize that we are especially susceptible to lust. This is why it's important to constantly guard our every thought and smallest action.

43. What is the difference between demonic possession and demonic oppression?

Vexation is a purely external attack. The demon may cause strange phenomena in a person's house, physically wound them, cause inexplicable illness, or cause obstacles in their professional or personal relationships. One may hear voices or experience visions. Some victims of oppression, such as Padre

Pio and John Vianney, were physically thrown around rooms, bludgeoned, and smeared with feces.

Obsession is an interior attack, in which the demon begins to assault his victim's mind. He may cause the person to become fixated on a single mental image, or he may implant feelings of depression or anger. In the worst cases, there is an inexplicable, pathological aversion to prayer and sacred objects.

Possession occurs when a demon physically takes up residence in one's body. There is a loss of consciousness, so the victim is not morally responsible for any deeds carried out by the demon inhabiting his body.

44. Do different demons have different "specialties"?

If you mean "Are some demons better at attacking nuns and others at attacking plumbers?" the answer is no.

They *do* have different calling cards, so to speak. Some are more talkative; others don't talk at all. Some are especially blasphemous; others are fonder of spitting. But, as Fr. Stanislaw says, none of them lack anything.

45. Are some demons more resilient than others?

Yes. Demons belong to the same hierarchy — the same order — in which they were created by God. So, the more high-ranking the demon, the harder he is to cast out. The names of the most powerful are well known. They include Lucifer, Beelzebub, Zebulun, Meridian, and Asmodeus.

46. Is it rare for an exorcist to encounter Lucifer himself, as Fr. Amorth did?

Satan is (of course) reluctant to subject himself to exorcism. When an exorcist begins to work on his patient, Satan will usually order one of the lesser angels to "take over" for him. So, the answer is: we don't know. But Lucifer is probably more involved in *particular cases* of demonic possession than can be verified.

47. Then how do exorcists know when he is involved?

Lucifer is extremely reluctant to identify himself, but when forced to, he will refer to himself simply as "I" — a blasphemous mimicry of God's "I Am."

48. Do demons act alone, or do they "hunt in packs"?

It varies from case to case. Every possession certainly begins with just one demon, but it is not unheard-of for ten or more demons to inhabit a single victim. The number of demons who attack the demoniac is usually tied to the spell cast by a wizard — that is, how many demons were invoked during the ritual.

49. Do demons only possess evildoers?

Not at all. In fact, they prefer innocent victims. The exorcist Fr. Faustino Negrini once asked a demon who was afflicting one of his flock — a fourteen-year-old girl — "Why did you choose her?" The devil replied, "Because she was the best in the parish."

50. What's the most common way that one becomes possessed?

Fr. Amorth's answer to this question is shocking:

> The most frequent case — and I put it at 90 percent — is that of the evil spell. It happens when someone sustains an evil caused by the demon that has been provoked by some person who has turned to Satan or someone who has acted with satanic perfidy. The remaining, 10 to 15 percent — I do not have an exact number — regard persons who have participated in occult practices, such as séances or satanic sects, or have contacted wizards or fortune-tellers.

So, the vast majority of demoniacs become oppressed or possessed principally through the malicious intent of another person.

51. Who would cast such a spell?

It may come as a nasty surprise, but family members are the most common culprits. According to Fr. Amorth:

> Jealous mothers view the daughter-in-law—particularly when there is an only son—as an enemy who is taking her beloved son from her. Very often the mothers-in-law become intrusive; they interfere in everything. In the worst cases, they order evil spells to the disadvantage of the daughters-in-law. I have exorcized many women whose spells were wished by their mothers-in-law.

The Maltese exorcist Fr. Elias Vella recalled a family being assailed by demons because the wife's mother cursed the gravy at Thanksgiving dinner!

52. What do those spells consist of?

Fr. Amorth believed they fall into six categories:

a. *Amatory*, in order to favor or destroy a romantic or love relationship.
b. *Venomous*, in order to procure a physical, psychic, economic, or familial evil.
c. *Binding*, in order to create impediments to actions, movements, or relationships.
d. *Transfer*, to transfer to a person the torments done to a puppet or a photo of the person.
e. *Putrefaction*, in order to procure a mortal evil by subjecting a material object to decay.

f. *Possession*, in order to introduce a diabolic presence in the victim and cause a true and proper possession.

53. So, the Catholic Church does believe in magic?

The old Catholic Encyclopedia defines magic as "the attempt to work miracles not by the power of God, gratuitously communicated to man, but by the use of hidden forces beyond man's control." We are forbidden from practicing magic in any form.

Most of those who think they are practicing magic are simply lying to themselves and others. By practicing this false magic, however, they are exposing themselves to demonic attacks. They are also starting down a dangerous course that leads to the evocation of demons.

True diabolists are given "magical" powers. That is, they are able to use the power of demons to perform supernatural feats that defy the laws of science (see question fifty-two). These are rare, however, and they come at a terrible cost to the diabolist himself.

54. How else can we invite demons into our own lives?

Unfortunately, many people actively seek to conjure demons. This is a ritual known as *evocation*; it is an important part of Satanism and other forms of diabolism. Any occult practice can lead to a demonic invasion, however. This is why the Catholic Church strictly prohibits us from using Ouija boards and tarot cards. We are also forbidden to practice palm reading and other methods of fortune telling.

55. Does the Church consider Reiki, homeopathy, and other forms of alternative medicine to be magic?

Reiki, yes; homeopathy, no. As Fr. Amorth explained:

> One cannot equate homeopathy with Reiki. Reiki of course is condemned. Homeopathy, when it is done with competence, is an alternative to official medicine and has the right to be looked at with respect and used with respect. I know many persons who are treated advantageously with

> homeopathic medicine. There is no danger when it is utilized by competent medical doctors and specialists, because it is only a treatment based on herbs — that is, on natural materials. Therefore, homeopathy is respectable.

56. What about meditation, yoga, and other Eastern practices? Do these also open one up to demons?

Catholics are encouraged to practice a particularly *Christian* form of meditation. Eucharistic adoration, the Holy Rosary, and *Lectio Divina* are the most common forms. Many spiritual masters have written extensively on this topic and have developed their own methods. These masters include Benedict of Nursia, Augustine of Hippo, Teresa of Ávila, and Ignatius of Loyola.

However, forms of meditation that are particular to non-Christian religions (such as yoga and transcendental meditation) are not to be practiced by Christians. We are forbidden to seek spiritual wisdom or enlightenment from non-Christian sources. On the other hand, to call these practices "gateway drugs" to diabolism would be overstating the case.

57. Are bad dreams a symptom of demonic oppression?

Surprisingly, this is rarely a sign of demonic affliction. It's not unheard-of, however. Fr. Amorth says, "One recognizes it from the fear that [such a dream] causes in the person. But if one invokes the name of Jesus and Mary, it goes away."

58. Why do some Christians blame rock music and the Harry Potter books for demonic activity?

Many rock musicians explicitly draw on satanic imagery, especially the pentagram, the "sign of the horns" (closing your fist, then raising your index and pinky fingers), and the number 666. This is a kind of "evil for the sake of evil" — in other words, Satanism. One may not personally believe in the devil, but this affection for evil opens up one's heart to demonic assault.

Meanwhile, exorcists criticize books such as *Harry Potter*, because glorification of magic lies at the center of every plot. This is in contrast to, for example, the legend of King Arthur or the *Lord of the Rings*. In such stories, wizards are secondary protagonists. The reader does not identify with Merlin or Gandalf the way he identifies with Harry Potter. He is therefore less tempted to toy with witchcraft.

59. Can places or houses be possessed?

Yes. Demons are particularly drawn to certain places: scenes of great evil, such as murders or Black Masses. It is possible that demons may choose to oppress certain locations as well as (or in addition to) certain people. When demons attack a certain place, it is known as a *demonic infestation*.

Localities that are under demonic infestation are known by supernatural happenings. Lights will turn on and off. There will be sudden, inexplicable explosions. Walls bleed.

However, there are locations so holy, so deeply imbued with God's grace, that the *places themselves* have the power to exorcise demons. The most powerful examples are scenes of Marian apparitions such as Loreto, Lourdes, and Fatima.

60. Can demons attack whole families?

It is possible. Some exorcists have reported encountering families in which both the parents of small children will suffer possession at the same time. It is a rare but horrible situation.

61. If someone sells his soul to the devil, can he ever get it back?

Everything that exists belongs to God, and that includes our souls. Our souls are not ours to "sell." So, even if we pledge ourselves to Satan — and even if he does some favor for us in return — God will always take us back.

62. Have any Satanists ever converted to Christianity?

Many have done so, but none is as famous as Bl. Bartolo Longo (1841–1926). Raised in a devout

Catholic household, Longo began to experiment with the occult when he was a college student. After a few years — and several encounters with the demonic — he was ordained a Satanic priest.

Eventually he returned to the Church, thanks in large part to the Holy Rosary, and he became a Third Order Dominican. He suffered from demonic attacks for the rest of his life but never wavered in his faith.

Longo was beatified by Pope St. John Paul II in 1980. His feast day is October 5.

PART THREE:

The Ministry of Exorcism

63. What is exorcism?

According to the *Catechism of the Catholic Church*, an exorcism is performed whenever "the Church asks publicly and authoritatively in the name of Jesus Christ that a person or object be protected against the power of the Evil One and withdrawn from his dominion" (paragraph 1673).

There are two kinds of exorcisms: major and minor.

Minor exorcisms are simple, commonplace prayers asking the power of God to free us from the oppression of sin and Hell. Minor exorcisms are performed at every Baptism, both for children and adults. Before Vatican II, parish priests would say prayers of exorcism over sacramentals such as blessed salt and holy water.

A *major exorcism* is a specific rite of the Church aimed at "the expulsion of demons or to the liberation from demonic possession" (*CCC*, paragraph 1673). This is what most people think of when they hear the word *exorcism*. Likewise, when we speak of *exorcists*, we mean priests who carry out major exorcisms. All bishops may serve as exorcists, but a priest must be appointed by his local ordinary before he can serve in the ministry of exorcism.

64. Isn't exorcism a relic of the Middle Ages?

Not at all. The Catholic Church does still practice exorcism — and, according to Fr. Amorth, the need for exorcists is growing every day:

> The ministry of exorcism remains an extremely important subject that should be imparted to all who are preparing for the priesthood, even more so, because so many young people are no longer going to Church, and instead are getting involved with séances, going to wizards, fortune tellers and so on. Therefore, I think that it is very important to inform them in order to keep them away from these dangers. And priests must be prepared to do the same....

> When, by chance, I happened to find myself before an evident case of diabolical possession, I understood that the reality of the satanic action and the prayer of liberation do not belong solely to the past, when Jesus practiced His ministry, but also to the present. Today, Satan is acting more than ever trying to lead as many souls as possible to an eternal death.

65. Hasn't science proven that demonic possession is a myth? Isn't that just what superstitious people used to call "mental illness"?

Certainly, many people suffering from mental illnesses have been mistaken for demoniacs. Fr. Amorth spoke of three "bestial" centuries of European history during which exorcisms became rare, and these poor souls were burned at the stake as witches rather than healed. Unfortunately, the same mistake is still made in less developed parts of the world. The Catholic Church makes her position perfectly clear, however:

> Illness, especially psychological illness, is a very different matter [from possession]; treating this

> is the concern of medical science. Therefore, before an exorcism is performed, it is important to ascertain that one is dealing with the presence of the Evil One, and not an illness. (*CCC*, paragraph 1673)

Therefore, all exorcists are now given special instruction to distinguish between mental and spiritual illness. If an exorcist determines that a patient does not suffer from demonic oppression or possession, he will routinely direct patients to a therapist or psychiatrist.

However, there's still a great need for "doctors" who tend to *spiritual* diseases. That's where the exorcists come in.

Also, the presence of mental illness does not totally exclude the possibility of demonic activity, and vice versa. In some cases, the spiritual attack causes deep psychological wounds. In others, the demons *stimulate* mental illness as a way of hurting their victims.

66. Who was the first exorcist?

Every ancient culture, including the Jews, had some kind of ritual for dispelling evil spirits. The first Christian exorcist, however, was Jesus! Our Lord performs several exorcisms in the Gospels. He also gave the Apostles — the first bishops — power to cast out demons (Luke 9:1). Catholics believe that this power is passed down through *apostolic succession* to every Catholic bishop in the world today. Bishops share that authority, known as exorcism, with these specially-trained priests.

67. Were exorcisms practiced in the early Church?

Yes! Church Fathers such as Athanasius, Cyprian, Irenaeus, and Tertullian wrote extensively about exorcism. Many elements of these earlier rites are still used by modern-day exorcists, including the invocation of the Sacred Name of Jesus, making the sign of the Cross, and breathing on the demoniac's face.

68. Does the Catholic Church accept the authority of non-Catholic exorcists?

The Catholic Church believes that anyone, anywhere, can pray for those who are oppressed or possessed by demons. Many non-Catholic Christians do exactly that.

These prayers may or may not bring about the desired effect. It's the same with Catholic exorcisms: it is God who drives out demons, not the exorcists themselves.

But the ministry of Catholic exorcists is more efficacious, because (a) they are authorized by the apostolic Church, and (b) they make use of valid sacramentals.

Even in the Orthodox Church, exorcisms are considered private prayers of deliverance. They are not part of a particular ministry with dedicated priests that perform specific rituals.

69. What about the false exorcists mentioned in Acts 19:13?

From the Church's very beginning, there have been many false exorcists. Most are simply con artists who prey on others' fears. Others are wizards themselves, and these "satanic exorcists" fall into two categories.

The first are those who believe that their pact with the devil gives them power over demons, thereby allowing them to perform real exorcisms. These people are delusional. *They* are under the power of demons. The demons may "obey" these false exorcists, in order to lead the diabolist (or the victim) into some greater evil, but for the most part, the demons will simply refuse to respond.

The second are those who present themselves as exorcists with the intention of casting further malignant spells, therefore strengthening the demons and causing even greater suffering to the victims and their families.

70. How are exorcists chosen?

According to the United States Conference of Catholic Bishops:

> As specified in canon 1172 §2 of the Code of Canon Law, the priest being appointed to the ministry of exorcist should possess piety, knowledge, prudence, and integrity of life. The Introduction to *Exorcisms and Related Supplications* further directs that the priest "has been specifically prepared for this office" (ERS, no. 13).

71. What are sacramentals, anyway, and why do exorcists use them?

Sacramentals are objects that have been blessed by a priest. They are, so to speak, conduits of grace. Exorcists use them because they channel God's power — much like the exorcist himself. There are three sacramentals use by virtually all exorcists:

> *Salt*. Blessed salt is used to protect a certain area from malignant spirits. Priests sprinkle blessed salt around the room before they begin their exorcism.

Oil. Blessed oil (chrism) is used to cure physical ailments, particularly those caused by demonic activity. This is applied directly to the demoniac's skin. Fr. Amorth would use it to bless his patients' senses: the forehead, eyes, nostrils, throat, mouth, and ears, tracing on the possessed the sign of the Cross.

Water. Surprisingly, the use of holy water in exorcisms is a more recent development. Still, it can be effective in blessing both places and people. Fr. Amorth recommended that those experiencing demonic attacks take small sips of holy water to defend themselves.

72. Is it true that the more sacramentals I use, the safer I will be?

No, because that's not how sacramentals work. Actually, sacramentals don't really "work" at all: God works *through* them. Hoarding sacramentals might lead us to believe that the objects themselves have some sort of innate power, which is a kind of idolatry or superstition.

73. Do Satanists have their own sacramentals?

Yes. When someone approaches a wizard or witch and asks for a spell, the diabolist will curse an object, such as an article of clothing or a piece of food. This is then given to the victim under false pretenses. They are somehow tricked into accepting the item. It may also be hidden in the victim's house — for instance, under a mattress or in the cushions of the couch.

At the beginning of an exorcism, the priest will try to identify the cursed object. If he succeeds in doing so, he will destroy it by burning it while praying for deliverance. This could be the deciding factor in whether the exorcism is successful or not.

74. Can only a priest be an exorcist?

Yes and no. It's true that only bishops and their authorized priests can officially perform major exorcisms. However, exorcists may invite laymen to serve as assistants. Also, anyone — priest, religious, or lay — can perform "minor exorcisms," or prayers of deliverance (see question sixty-three).

75. How are exorcists trained?

Fr. Amorth was adamant that a purely academic study is worthless in preparing one for the ministry. "The school of exorcism is practical experience," he said. There is some study, but only hands-on practice can prepare a newcomer for the ministry. It's rather like an apprentice system. New exorcists are assigned to an experienced practitioner. They will assist the veteran exorcist at hundreds of exorcisms before "going solo."

76. How many exorcists are there in the Catholic Church?

Not enough. In theory, there should be at least one per diocese. Today, however, there are sometimes whole countries in Europe that don't have a single exorcist. Part of this is due to the worldwide shortage of priests. But, according to Fr. Amorth, it's not the only reason:

> One leaves the seminary and becomes a priest without ever having heard anyone speak of the devil or exorcisms, of the danger of wizards and other occult sciences; or of diabolical possession.

> And then not believing in any of it, he never preaches it. I have had so many priests come to assist at my exorcisms say, "Look, Fr. Amorth, before I did not believe — now I believe!"

77. Will a Catholic exorcist treat a non-Catholic patient?

Absolutely. The only thing required of a patient is a belief that by cooperating with the exorcist, God will liberate her from her demons. No doctrinal test is administered. In fact, Fr. Amorth often worked with patients who kept their meetings a secret, because they were embarrassed to be seen with a Catholic priest!

Father found these experiences heartening, however. The patient's acknowledgment of supernatural evil at work in her life, combined with an understanding that a priest was her only true recourse, was evidence of the rudiments of faith. Of course, many of Fr. Amorth's patients converted to Catholicism after their firsthand experiences of spiritual warfare.

78. Who is the patron saint of exorcists?

Many exorcists have been canonized, including Anthony of Egypt, John of the Cross, and Francis Borgia. The patron saint of exorcists, however, is Benedict of Nursia. Though not a priest himself, Benedict was adept at driving out demons by using intercessory prayer.

79. What is the St. Benedict Medal?

According to the Benedictine Center, the Medal of St. Benedict is itself "a prayer of exorcism against Satan." There are so many symbols contained in the remarkable image it bears, but the symbol most relevant to this book is the letters etched into the arms of the Cross. They stand for: *Crux sacra sit mihi lux! Nunquam draco sit mihi dux!* This is an ancient prayer of exorcism. Both because of its symbolism and because of Benedict's patronage, the St. Benedict Medal is the sacramental most commonly associated with protection against the demonic.

80. What are the most common "gateway sins" that lead to demonic activity?

According to Fr. Amorth, violations of the sixth commandment — that is, sins of impurity — are almost always involved in demonic activity:

> This is not the most serious sin, but it is our weakness. The most serious sins are those of arrogance and pride. But the violation of the sixth commandment is also the most common sin, so that St. Alphonsus Liguori said, "One goes to Hell either for this sin, or not without this sin." Everyone sins against this commandment. It is our greatest weakness.

81. Are some exorcists better than others?

Yes and no. When asked this question, Fr. Amorth replied:

> I do not deny that there are differences between one exorcist and another. But what the differences *are* is always difficult to evaluate. There are spiritual factors, for example, the intensity of prayer, the union with God and sacrifices; and then there are human factors like experience, intelligence, a specific culture and intuition.

> But often everything is relative. Some exorcists function better with certain demons and not so well with others.

82. Where does the exorcist get his powers?

Strictly speaking, exorcists have no special powers. They simply use prayers and sacramentals (such as holy water) to deliver patients from demons. They are vehicles of God's grace and nothing more. So, there's no way to guarantee that *any* exorcism will be successful. God liberates the soul in His own time and by the means of His choosing.

For example, Padre Pio was given a special grace to discern whether demoniacs were "mature" enough to be liberated from their demons. When he encountered a demoniac whose moment of liberation (as appointed by God) had not yet come, he would give her a blessing and send her on her way. There was nothing else he could do, because all his power came from God.

Conversely, some of the worst cases of possession can be "cured" almost instantaneously. Padre Pio was also known to speak a few words to a demoniac ("go away from him"), and the demon would instantly depart.

83. Where are exorcisms performed?

Contrary to what you see in Hollywood films, the Church strongly discourages exorcists from practicing their ministry in the patient's home. Fr. Amorth's protocol is the correct one: an exorcist should have an office or a small chapel — one far away from the street, so the public cannot hear the demon shouting and screaming.

84. What can an exorcist do if a demoniac doesn't want to be exorcized?

Not much, unfortunately. A victim of demonic oppression and possession must desire freedom from Satan. He must be an active participant in the exorcism process. He must bend whatever willpower he still possesses against the demon that is invading his body. If he is unwilling to resist the demon — whether it's because he is a Satanist or simply because he's lazy — the exorcism will not succeed.

On the other hand, St. Alphonsus Liguori said, "One is not always able to liberate a person from diabolical possession. But one is always able to give some relief." For those willing to be exorcized, this relief is a blessing in itself. For the unwilling, it may create an opening for the Lord to change their hearts and make them open to the healing ministry offered by exorcists.

So, even if a patient is unwilling, an exorcist will still do everything in his power to free him or her. There are no hopeless cases.

And in some rare instances, holy men and women will ask God *not* to liberate them from their demons. According to Fr. Amorth, these persons "offer themselves as victims":

> I think of a nun who was possessed by the devil and was never liberated. She offered all her tremendous suffering for the souls in purgatory, for the conversion of sinners, and for her spiritual children, the same goals Jesus had when dying on the Cross. All these sufferings offered to God have great value.

85. Is there truth in the Hollywood depictions of exorcisms — green skin, projectile vomiting, and so forth?

Absolutely. Fr. Amorth encountered these horrors every day:

> There are very many who spit, and they try to guess the exact moment to get you. An exorcist with a little experience learns to defend himself from the spitting; he knows about it, and he tries to put a handkerchief or tissue in front of his face. Anyhow, I recall one who always spit, and I would see it coming in time, so I would put a hand in front of my mouth. Once, as he spit, three nails materialized in his mouth. I still have those nails. I keep them in my room on the third floor. Sometimes I bring these objects on television, because television needs props, needs to show things.

86. Do demons only oppress people, or can they also infect objects?

They can oppress both. Demons will use any means at their disposal to frighten or hurt their victims. Exorcists commonly report objects falling off walls or flying around the room in the presence of a demon.

These demons' powers extend far beyond the proximity of their victims. Once, when the exorcist Fr. Faustino Negrini was taking a patient to see Padre Pio, the car repeatedly died on the road. "The driver would look under the hood, and everything was fine, there was no problem. Then Fr. Faustino would pray and do exorcisms, and the car would function again, and the demon would laugh."

87. Are exorcisms performed ex opere operaro?

This phrase means "from the work performed" and refers to the sacramental ministry of the priesthood. For instance, as long as the legitimate *form* of the Eucharist (the prayers of consecration) and *matter* (bread and wine) are joined with the proper *intent* by the priest (to affect transubstantiation in the person of Christ), a valid Eucharist is confected. This work is performed whether the priest is a saint or barely clings to his faith.

Exorcisms are not like that. The more faith an exorcist brings to the table, the more effective he will be. This is why the mere presence of some saints has been enough to drive out demons (see question ninety-three).

88. How does one find an exorcist?

One should approach the nearest Catholic priest or the diocesan chancery (headquarters). He or she will be able to locate the priest who has been appointed to the ministry of exorcism. Sometimes, the local ordinary (bishop) will perform exorcisms personally.

If one's local diocese does not have an official exorcist — which is the case in too many parts of the world today — the demoniac may have to travel to different parts of the country, or even different continents, to find a licit exorcist.

89. Why are the identities of exorcists kept secret?

The Church does not teach that exorcism is, by its nature, a secretive ministry. She simply recommends that exorcists remain anonymous, for two reasons.

The first is to keep the priest from being inundated with dubious requests. Exorcisms must always be conducted with the approval of the local bishop. If the identity of the diocese's exorcist is unknown, seekers have no choice but to approach the chancery.

The second is to protect the patient's identity.

Therefore, those who do speak openly about their ministry of healing — such as Fr. Amorth, Fr. Chad Ripperger, Msgr. Stephen Rossetti, and others — are not doing anything wrong. On the contrary, it is necessary that the public become more aware of this ministry.

90. Do exorcists live by a certain rule of life, as monks do?

The Church calls exorcists to lives of extraordinary prayer and fasting. Otherwise, no. They do not have a "rule," like the Rule of St. Augustine or the Rule of St. Benedict.

91. Do exorcisms have to be performed in person?

No. Exorcisms (or parts of exorcisms) can also be performed by telephone. Some modern exorcists use Skype! This seems odd, but Fr. Amorth said, "The fundamental mainstay of the exorcist is prayer made with faith, not the place or the way it is done." Father Stanislaw concurred, "An exorcism done at a distance has the same efficacy as that done in the exorcist's presence."

92. Are the elaborate rituals necessary?

Not strictly speaking. St. Paul of the Cross — the founder of the Passionists — could exorcize demons by making the sign of the Cross. Don Bosco once healed a demoniac simply by approaching her when he was dressed in his sacred vestments and preparing for Mass. But this is a rare charism. Most exorcists are required to use the more elaborate prayer ceremonies.

93. Why are demons so repelled by images of Pope St. John Paul II?

John Paul II was the first pope in four hundred years to carry out an exorcism. In fact, he carried out two! After the first experience, John Paul II confided in a cardinal, "I've never had anything like this happen to me in my life.... Everything that happens in the Gospels still happens today."

94. Do exorcists ever abuse their office?

Unfortunately, inevitably, they do. It is not unheard-of that an exorcist will sexually abuse his own patients. This is one of the most terrible sins imaginable. It is also a great help and comfort to the demons! This is why the Church requires that an exorcist never be alone with a patient. If the patient is female, one of the other parties present must also be a woman.

95. What can the laity do to help those afflicted by demonic activity?

Fr. Amorth taught that all laymen could perform "prayers of liberation" — which, "when done with faith, are as effective as true and proper exorcisms." According to Father:

> When a priest prays a public prayer of liberation, he is not carrying out initiatives performed by the exorcist in order to liberate a person from the devil; rather, he is praying a private prayer, the prayer given by Jesus, that all can pray.

Father also said prayers of praise and gratitude are extremely effective, as are the Psalms.

96. Do demons make a point of attacking exorcists?

If so, they fail. Exorcists are given special protection from God. To put it another way, exorcists are *less* likely to suffer from demonic vexation, oppression, or possession than ordinary Catholics.

97. Do Satanists have "counter-exorcists"?

They do. This is actually a large part of the reason why exorcisms are practiced in secret. The wizards and witches who cast evil spells may attend a public exorcism (or healing Mass or prayer service) and "unload negativity," as Fr. Stanislaw put it. These "mysterious rites" serve to reinforce the demon possessing the victim.

98. Who should pray these prayers of liberation?

Everyone! St. Peter warns us, "Your adversary the devil prowls around like a roaring lion, seeking some one to devour" (1 Peter 5:8). Spiritual warfare is part of the ordinary life of a Christian. That is why Fr. Amorth urged us always to have prayers of liberation on our lips. One of his favorites was "In the name of Jesus, go away!"

99. Does the Church recommend any specific prayers for laymen?

Yes. There is an official Prayer for Deliverance that is approved for the laity. It says:

> My Lord, You are all powerful, You are God, You are Father.
>
> We beg You through the intercession and help of the archangels Michael, Raphael, and Gabriel, for the deliverance of our brothers and sisters who are enslaved by the evil one.
>
> All saints of Heaven, come to our aid.
>
> From anxiety, sadness, and obsessions,
>
> We beg You, free us, O Lord.
> From hatred, fornication, envy,
>
> We beg You, free us, O Lord.
> From thoughts of jealousy, rage, and death,
>
> We beg You, free us, O Lord.
> From every thought of suicide and abortion,
>
> We beg You, free us, O Lord.
> From every form of sinful sexuality,

We beg You, free us, O Lord.
From every division in our family, and every harmful friendship,

We beg You, free us, O Lord.
From every sort of spell, malefic, witchcraft, and every form of the occult,

We beg You, free us, O Lord.

100. What is the most effective way of defending oneself from demonic attacks?

Fr. Amorth recommended calling upon your guardian angel for protection. Your angel has experience in fighting the devil; he will struggle to defend you until your final breath!

However, many experts (including Fr. Amorth) believed that it was nearly impossible for a full-blown Satanist to repent — not because God would not accept him, but because his will was so bent towards evil and his mind so corrupted by the devil that he would never be able to humble himself and repent.

101. If one is liberated from a demon, can one's life ever go back to normal?

No — but that's not necessarily a bad thing. While many former demoniacs bear mental and spiritual scars for the rest of their lives, there are actually some benefits.

For nonbelievers and their families, their experience (oppression, vexation, or possession) serves as supernatural confirmation of the truth of Christianity. As discussed in question seventy-eight, these demons have accidentally saved souls for Christ by proving the existence of the devil! For believers, the experience of liberation from a demon leaves one with a lasting gratitude for Jesus, Our Lady, and the ministry of the Church.

Either way, thousands of souls have surely gone to Heaven that otherwise would have gone to Hell, if only the devil had left them alone.

Short Biography of Fr. Amorth

Fr. Gabriele Amorth (1925–2016), the most famous Italian exorcist, was ordained a priest in 1954. In 1985, he became an exorcist for the Diocese of Rome, a ministry he practiced until he died. In 1990, he founded the International Association of Exorcists, of which he was president until 2000. He wrote more than thirty books in Italian, many of which have been translated into other languages. His other works published by Sophia Institute Press are: *The Devil is Afraid of Me*, *An Exorcist Explains the Demonic*, and *Father Amorth: My Battle against Satan*.

Resources

The following resources may be found on the Internet using one of the search engines or at your local Catholic bookstore.

Adult Faith Formation Programs

- https://avila-institute.org/spiritual-formation/ — features a course on Catholic spirituality including an offering on "Angels and Demons," "Discerning Spirits," and "Spiritual Warfare in Modern Times: C.S. Lewis and *The Screwtape Letters*."
- https://mnehealing.org/ — Missionaries of the New Evangelization provides training in healing and deliverance for priests and seminarians.
- https://www.omvusa.org/our-work/virtual-workshops/overcoming-spiritual-discouragement/ — Fr. Timothy Gallagher, O.M.V.'s free virtual workshop on "Overcoming Spiritual Discouragement."

Books/Articles/Audios/Videos

Unless otherwise indicated, all of the following materials are books. Many of the titles are available from Sophia Institute Press.

Fr. Gabriele Amorth (related works)

- ✠ *An Exorcist Explains the Demonic: The Antics of Satan and His Army of Fallen Angels*
- ✠ *The Devil is Afraid of Me: The Life and Work of the World's Most Popular Exorcist*
- ✠ *Father Amorth: My Battle Against Satan*
- ✠ *Padre Pio: Stories and Memories of My Mentor and Friend*

Angels

For Adults:

- ✠ *Angels and Their Mission,* Jean Danielou
- ✠ *Encounters with Angels: The Invisible Companions of Our Spiritual Life,* Odile Haumonte
- ✠ *His Angels at Our Side: Understanding Their Power in our Souls and in the World,* Fr. John Horgan
- ✠ *Mother Angelica on God, His Home, and His Angels,* Mother Mary Angelica

For Children:

- ✠ *A Book of Angels,* Marigold Hunt
- ✠ *How the Angels Got Their Wings,* Anthony DeStefano

Church Teachings on Satan and Evil

- ✠ *The Devil in the Castle,* Dan Burke
- ✠ *Evidence of Satan in the Modern World,* Léon Cristiani
- ✠ *The Screwtape Letters,* C.S. Lewis
- ✠ *The Snakebite Letters,* Peter Kreeft
- ✠ *Who is the Devil?,* Nicolas Corte

- *Why Does God Permit Evil?,* Dom Bruno Webb
- *The Wrath of God: How to Read the Signs of the Times and Recognize the Evils of Our Age,* Fr. Livio Fanzaga*

Private Revelations

Note: Although the Catholic Church accepts many private revelations, readers should always proceed with caution — private revelations are not part of the official deposit of Catholic teaching and may contain theological errors. Before reading materials containing private revelations, first read the book *A Still, Small Voice* by Fr. Benedict Groeschel.

Discernment

- *Spiritual Warfare and Discernment of Spirits,* Dan Burke
- *The Catholic Guide to Miracles: Separating the Authentic from the Counterfeit,* Adam Blai
- *Discernment of Spirits in Marriage: Ignatian Wisdom for Husbands and Wives,* Fr. Timothy Gallagher
- *The Discernment of Spirits: An Ignatian Guide for Everyday Living,* Fr. Timothy Gallagher
- *Overcoming Spiritual Discouragement: The Wisdom and Power of Venerable Bruno Lanteri,* Fr. Timothy Gallagher
- *Struggles in the Spiritual Life: Their Nature and Remedies,* Fr. Timothy Gallagher**
- *Understanding Miracles: How to Know if They Are from God, the Devil, or the Imagination,* Zsolt Aradi

**Fr. Timothy Gallagher also has a free video series that may be viewed on Discerning Hearts and his website has further resources on discernment of spirits at frtimothygallagher.org

Exorcism

- ✠ *Diary of an American Exorcist: Demons, Possession, and the Modern-Day Battle Against Ancient Evil,* Msgr. Stephen Rossetti
- ✠ *Exorcism: The Battle Against Satan and His Demons*, Fr. Vincent P. Lampert
- ✠ *Exorcism: Encounters with the Paranormal and the Occult,* Fr. Jose Francisco C. Syquia
- ✠ *The Exorcism Files: True Stories of Demonic Possession,* Adam Blai
- ✠ *An Exorcist Explains How to Heal the Possessed and Help Souls Suffering Spiritual Crises,* Fr. Paolo Carlin
- ✠ *Exorcist Volume Two: Spiritual Battle Lines,* Fr. Jose Francisco C. Syquia
- ✠ *Exorcist Volume Three: Spiritual Warfare and Discernment,* Fr. Jose Francisco C. Syquia
- ✠ *The Exorcist Files,* interviews by Joy L. Cuadrante, edited by Fr. Jose Francisco C. Syquia

Overcoming Sin

- ✠ *Idol Thoughts,* Fr. Denis Lemieux
- ✠ *Manual for Conquering Deadly Sin,* Fr. Dennis Kolinski, S.J.C.

- *Overcoming the Evil Within: The Reality of Sin and the Transforming Power of God's Grace and Mercy,* Fr. Wade Menezes
- *Overcoming Sinful Anger: How to Master Your Emotions and Bring Peace to Your Life,* Fr. Thomas Morrow
- *Overcoming Sinful Thoughts: How to Realign Your Thinking and Defeat Harmful Ideas,* Fr. Thomas Morrow
- *Rooting Out Hidden Faults: What is the Particular Examen, and How Does It Conquer Sin?,* Fr. James F. McElhone, C.S.C.
- *The Seven Deadly Sins: Thomistic Guide to Vanquishing Vice and Sin,* Kevin Vost, Psy.D.

Prayer Books for Protection and Deliverance

- *Deliverance Prayers: For Use by the Laity,* Fr. Chad A. Ripperberger, Ph.D.
- *The Rosary: Your Weapon for Spiritual Warfare,* Johnette Benkovic and Thomas K. Sullivan
- *The Warrior's Rosary: Meditations for Spiritual Combat,* Johnette Benkovic and Thomas K. Sullivan
- *Catholic Handbook of Deliverance Prayers,* Fr. Jose Francisco C. Syquia
- *True Knights: Combat Training Daily Prayers for Purity,* Kenneth Henderson and Jesse Romero (editors)

Saints Against Temptation and Evil

- *The Curé of Ars: Patron Saint of Parish Priests,* Fr. Bartholomew O'Brien
- *The Diary of St. Gemma,* St. Gemma Galgani

- ✠ *Miracles of John Paul II,* Pawel Zuchniewicz
- ✠ *St. Anthony of the Desert,* St. Athanasius

Spiritual Healing and Growth

- ✠ *The Fulfillment of All Desire,* Ralph Martin
- ✠ *God's Healing Mercy: Finding Your Path to Forgiveness, Peace, and Joy*, Kathleen Beckman
- ✠ *Healing Your Family Tree,* Fr. John Hampsch, C.M.F.
- ✠ *Women Made New: Reflections on Adversity, Transformation, and Healing,* Crystalina Evert

Spiritual Warfare

- ✠ *The Art of Spiritual Warfare: The Secret Weapons Satan Can't Withstand,* Venatius Oforka
- ✠ *Catholics, Wake Up!: Be a Spiritual Warrior,* Jesse Romero
- ✠ *Christ and the Powers of Darkness,* Fr. J. Godfrey Raupert
- ✠ *The Deceiver: Our Daily Struggle with Satan,* Fr. Livio Fanzaga
- ✠ *Devil in the Castle: St. Teresa of Avila, Spiritual Warfare, and the Progress of the Soul,* Dan Burke
- ✠ *The Devil in the City of Angels: My Encounters with the Diabolical,* Jesse Romero
- ✠ *Dominion: The Nature of Diabolic Warfare,* Fr. Chad A. Ripperberger
- ✠ *A Family Guide to Spiritual Warfare: Strategies for Deliverance and Healing,* Kathleen Beckman
- ✠ *Immortal Combat: Confronting the Heart of Darkness,* Fr. Dwight Longenecker
- ✠ *Lord, Prepare My Hands for Battle,* Jesse Romero

- ✠ *Queen of Militants,* Emil Neubert, S., S.T.D.
- ✠ *Manual for Spiritual Warfare,* Paul Thigpen
- ✠ *Spiritual Combat: How to Win Your Spiritual Battles and Attain Inner Peace,* Lorenzo Scupoli
- ✠ *Spiritual Warfare and the Discernment of Spirits,* Dan Burke

Internet Resources

Catholic Faith — General

- ✠ www.catholiceducation.org — offers a resource library which includes articles on Church teachings regarding evil and spiritual warfare
- ✠ www.catholicexchange.com — *the* Catholic homepage on the Web, which offers articles, podcasts, and other tools for spiritual growth
- ✠ www.crossroadsinitiative.com — a Catholic education and evangelization apostolate
- ✠ https://opusangelorum.org/ — Opus Santorum Angelorum (Work of the Holy Angels) provides catechesis on the angels, prayers, and their role in our lives
- ✠ www.spiritualdirection.com — a Catholic site for spiritual education and formation
- ✠ www.stpaulcenter.com — includes resources on exorcism, deliverance, and spiritual warfare
- ✠ https://www.womenofgrace.com/ — offers ongoing spiritual formation and resources on various topics, including the dangers of New Age practices

Broadcast Media

- www.discerninghearts.com — free Catholic podcasts including programs from Dan Burke on "St. Teresa of Avila and Spiritual Warfare"; Fr. Timothy Gallagher, O.M.V. on "The Discernment of Spirits and more" and "Spiritual Desolation"; Fr. Robert Spitzer, S.J. on "The Light Shines on in the Darkness"; and Paul Thigpen on "A Manual for Spiritual Warfare."
- Eternal Word Television Network — www.ewtn.com
- Relevant Radio (Starboard Network) — www.relevantradio.com

Prayers

Prayer for Deliverance

My Lord, You are all powerful, You are God, You are Father. We beg You through the intercession and help of the archangels Michael, Raphael and Gabriel, for the deliverance of our brothers and sisters who are enslaved by the evil one. All saints of Heaven, come to our aid.

From anxiety, sadness, and obsessions,
  We beg You, free us, O Lord.

From hatred, fornication, envy,
  We beg You, free us, O Lord.

From thoughts of jealousy, rage, and death,
  We beg You, free us, O Lord.

From every thought of suicide and abortion,
  We beg You, free us, O Lord.

From every form of sinful sexuality,
    We beg You, free us, O Lord.

From every division in our family, and every
    harmful friendship,
    We beg You, free us, O Lord.

From every sort of spell, malefic, witchcraft,
    and every form of the occult,
    We beg You, free us, O Lord.

Lord, You Who said, "I leave you peace, My peace I give you," grant that, through the intercession of the Virgin Mary, we may be liberated from every evil spell and enjoy Your peace always. In the name of Christ, our Lord. Amen.

Prayer to St. Michael the Archangel

St. Michael the Archangel, defend us in battle. Be our protection against the wickedness and snares of the devil; May God rebuke him, we humbly pray; And do thou, O Prince of the Heavenly Host, by the power of God, thrust into hell Satan and all evil spirits who wander through the world for the ruin of souls. Amen.

Sophia Institute

Sophia Institute is a nonprofit institution that seeks to nurture the spiritual, moral, and cultural life of souls and to spread the Gospel of Christ in conformity with the authentic teachings of the Roman Catholic Church.

Sophia Institute Press fulfills this mission by offering translations, reprints, and new publications that afford readers a rich source of the enduring wisdom of mankind.

Sophia Institute also operates the popular online Catholic resource CatholicExchange.com. *Catholic Exchange* provides world news from a Catholic perspective as well as daily devotionals and articles that will help readers to grow in holiness and live a life consistent with the teachings of the Church.

In 2013, Sophia Institute launched Sophia Institute for Teachers to renew and rebuild Catholic culture through service to Catholic education. With the goal of nurturing the spiritual, moral, and cultural life of souls, and an abiding respect for the role and work of teachers, we strive to provide materials and programs that are at once enlightening to the mind and ennobling to the heart; faithful and complete, as well as useful and practical.

Sophia Institute gratefully recognizes the Solidarity Association for preserving and encouraging the growth of our apostolate over the course of many years. Without their generous and timely support, this book would not be in your hands.

www.SophiaInstitute.com
www.CatholicExchange.com
www.SophiaInstituteforTeachers.org

Sophia Institute Press® is a registered trademark of Sophia Institute.
Sophia Institute is a tax-exempt institution as defined by the Internal Revenue Code, Section 501(c)(3). Tax I.D. 22-2548708.